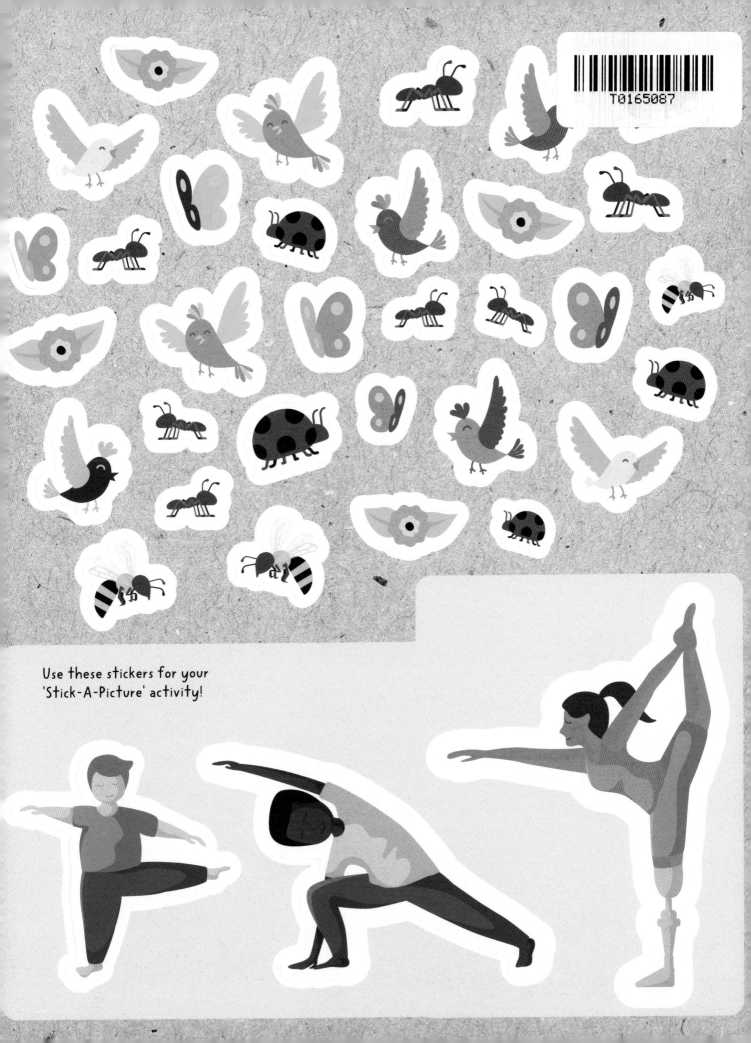

Use these stickers for your
'Stick-A-Picture' activity!

SMALL STEPS *for* BIG CHANGE

STICKER
ACTIVITY
Book

FIVE M.LE

WHICH BIN?

Use your sticker to label
which bin is recycling!

What can I recycle?

Glass bottles
and jars

Paper,
cartons and
cardboard

Metal
cans

Plastic
bottles, tubs,
jugs and
jars

COMPOST ME!

Circle the foods that you can compost below.

what can I compost?

Fruit and vegetable scraps

Stale or mouldy bread

Coffee grounds and tea bags/ leaves

Fresh grass, plants, stalks and flowers

HEALTHY, HAPPY PLATE!

Use your stickers to add healthy fruits
and vegetables to the plate below!

WHICH WAY?

Help the worm through the maze to the surface!

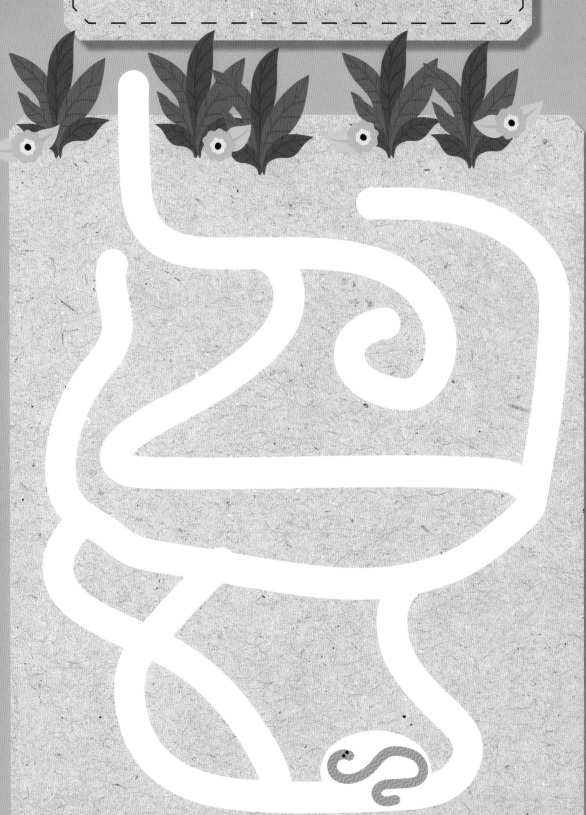

HOW DOES YOUR GARDEN GROW?

Use your stickers to fill this garden with flowers, bees and veggies!

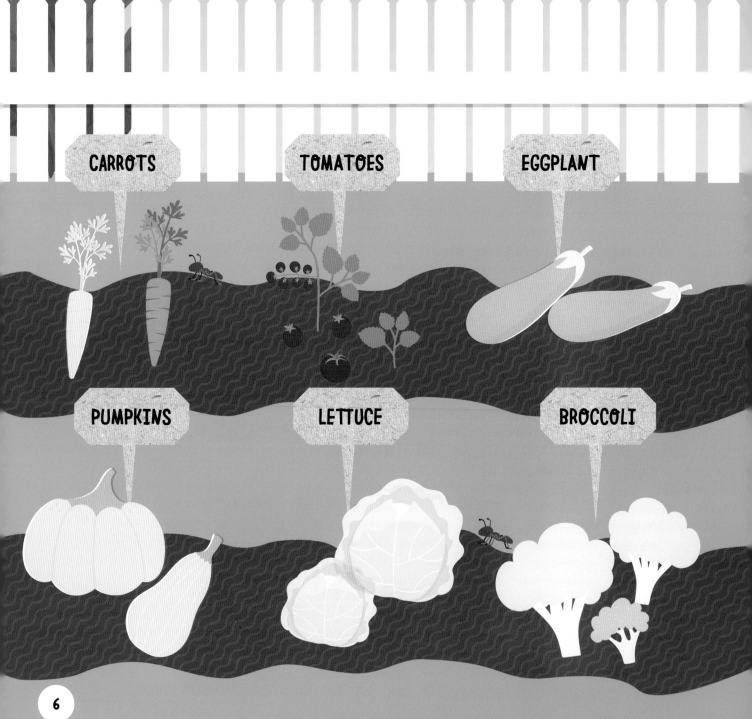

CARROTS

TOMATOES

EGGPLANT

PUMPKINS

LETTUCE

BROCCOLI

HOW MANY?

Count how many ants are marching into their hill!

THERE ARE _____ ANTS

BUZZING BEE

Help the bee get his nectar
back to the hive!

START

FINISH

DRAW BY GRID

Use the grid below to help
you draw the dragonfly.

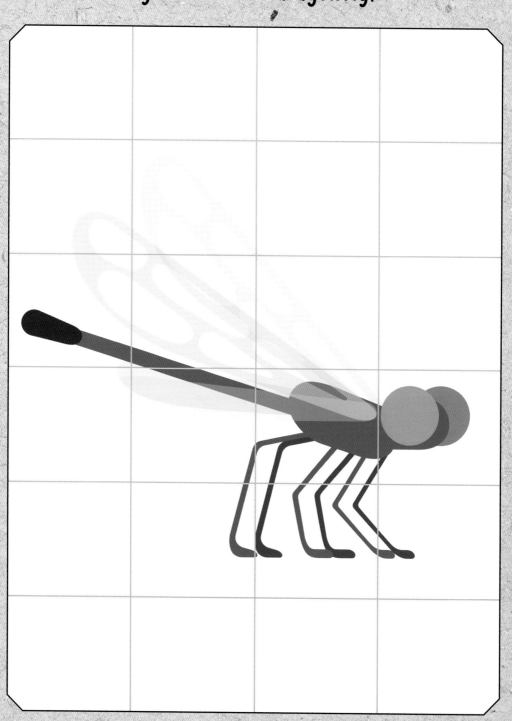

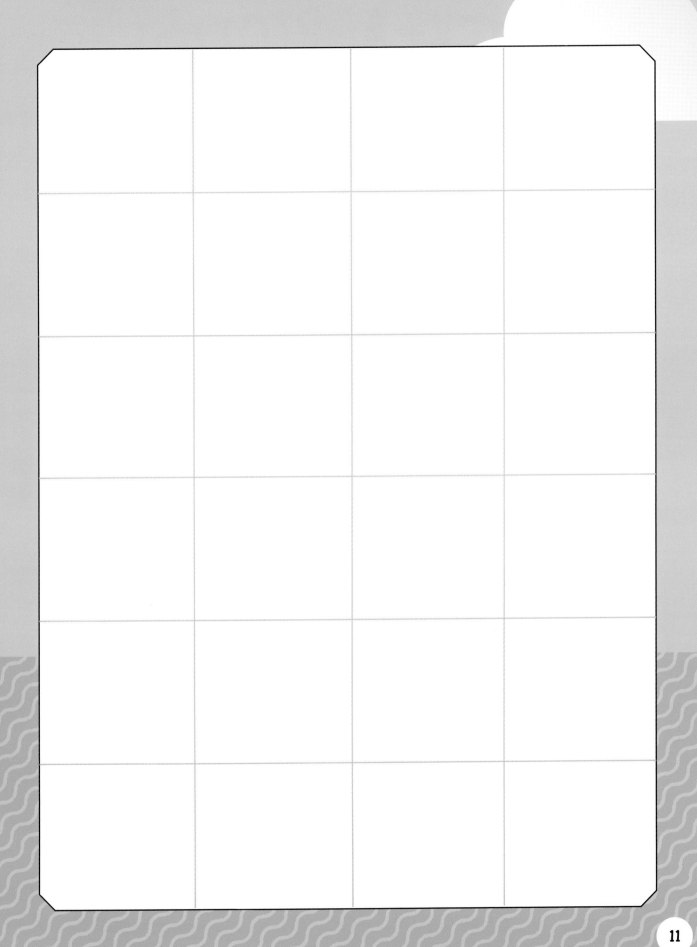

STICK-A-PICTURE

Use your stickers to finish
the pictures below of people
moving their bodies!

MINDFUL COLOURING

Use your favourite pencils
to colour in the mandala!

I AM GRATEFUL FOR ...

Draw some of the things you are
grateful for in the hearts below!

ANSWERS

Page 2: Which Bin?

Page 8: How Many?
There are 10 ants.

Page 9: Buzzing Bee

Page 3: Compost Me!

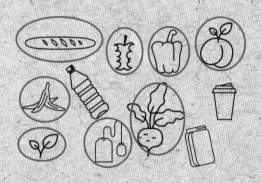

Page 5: Which Way?